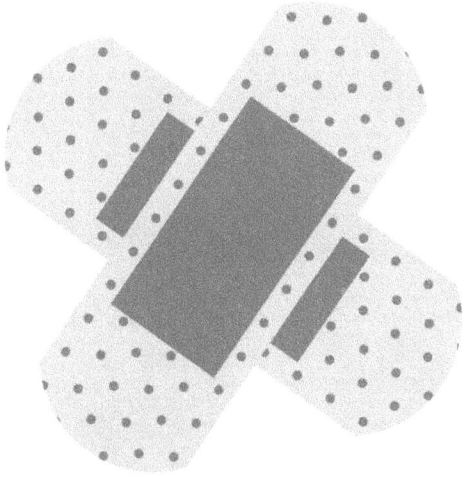

IF SURVIVAL LOG IS FOUND

please return to:

_____

DEDICATION

This Survival Journal is dedicated to all the people out there who love to prepare for their wilderness adventures and document their findings in the process.

You are my inspiration for producing books and I'm honored to be a part of keeping all of your Survival Checklist notes and records organized.

This journal notebook will help you record your details about your wilderness adventures.

Thoughtfully put together with these sections to record: Date, Conditions, Shelter, Food Inventory, Journey, Map Sketch, and Party Members.

HOW TO USE THIS BOOK

The purpose of this book is to keep all of your Survival checklist notes all in one place. It will help keep you organized.

This Survival Journal Book will allow you to accurately document every detail about maintaining your wilderness adventures. It's a great way to chart your course through a surviving in the wild.

Here are examples of the prompts for you to fill in and write about your experience in this book:

1. Date - Write the date.

2. Conditions - Log the conditions for the weather and the terrain.

3. Shelter - Record details about your shelter: Constructed, Type, Coverings, Waterproof, Animal Proof, Sunproof, Fire Started.

4. Food Inventory - Write about your food including: Rations, Water, Hunted, Fished, Foraging.

5. Journey - Log the Distance Covered, Trail Markers Used, Landmarks Sighted, Animal Prints.

6. Map Sketch - Record the Latitude, Longitude Location.

7. Party Members - Write the names of the members in your party including Status, Injuries, Treatment.

Date _____

Conditions

Weather

Terrain

Shelter

Shelter Constructed ☐

Type of Shelter

_____

_____

_____

Clothing/Coverings ☐

Waterproof ☐

Animal proof ☐

Sunproof ☐

Fire Started ☐

Food Inventory

Rations ☐

_____

_____

_____

_____

Water ☐

Hunting ☐

_____

_____

Fishing ☐

_____

_____

Foraging ☐

_____

_____

Journey

Distance Covered

Trail Markers Used

Landmarks Sighted

Animal Prints

Map Sketch

Lat.   Long.

Party Member	Status	Injuries	Treatment

Date _____

Conditions

Weather

Terrain

Shelter

Shelter Constructed ☐

Type of Shelter

_____

_____

_____

Clothing/Coverings ☐

Waterproof ☐

Animal proof ☐

Sunproof ☐

Fire Started ☐

Food Inventory

Rations ☐

_____

_____

_____

_____

Water ☐

Hunting ☐

_____

_____

_____

Fishing ☐

_____

_____

_____

Foraging ☐

_____

_____

_____

Journey

Distance Covered

Trail Markers Used

Landmarks Sighted

Animal Prints

Map Sketch

Lat.   Long.

Party Member	Status	Injuries	Treatment

Date _____

Conditions

Weather

Terrain

Shelter

Shelter Constructed ☐

Type of Shelter

_____

_____

_____

Clothing/Coverings ☐

Waterproof ☐

Animal proof ☐

Sunproof ☐

Fire Started ☐

Food Inventory

Rations ☐

_____

_____

_____

_____

Water ☐

Hunting ☐

_____

_____

_____

Fishing ☐

_____

_____

_____

Foraging ☐

_____

_____

_____

Journey

Distance Covered

Trail Markers Used

Landmarks Sighted

Animal Prints

Map Sketch

Lat.　　　Long.

Party Member	Status	Injuries	Treatment

Date _____

Conditions

Weather

Terrain

Shelter

Shelter Constructed ☐

Type of Shelter

_____

_____

_____

Clothing/Coverings ☐

Waterproof ☐

Animal proof ☐

Sunproof ☐

Fire Started ☐

Food Inventory

Rations ☐

_____

_____

_____

_____

Water ☐

Hunting ☐

_____

_____

_____

Fishing ☐

_____

_____

_____

Foraging ☐

_____

_____

_____

Journey

Distance Covered

Trail Markers Used

Landmarks Sighted

Animal Prints

Map Sketch

Lat. Long.

Party Member	Status	Injuries	Treatment

Date _____

Conditions

Weather

Terrain

Shelter

Shelter Constructed ☐

Type of Shelter

_____

_____

Clothing/Coverings ☐

Waterproof ☐

Animal proof ☐

Sunproof ☐

Fire Started ☐

Map Sketch

Lat.   Long.

Food Inventory

Rations ☐

_____
_____
_____
_____

Water ☐

Hunting ☐

_____
_____
_____

Fishing ☐

_____
_____
_____

Foraging ☐

_____
_____
_____

Journey

Distance Covered

Trail Markers Used

Landmarks Sighted

Animal Prints

Party Member	Status	Injuries	Treatment

Date _____

Conditions

Weather

Terrain

Shelter

Shelter Constructed ☐

Type of Shelter

_____

_____

Clothing/Coverings ☐
Waterproof ☐
Animal proof ☐
Sunproof ☐
Fire Started ☐

Food Inventory

Rations ☐

_____
_____
_____
_____

Water ☐
Hunting ☐

_____
_____
_____

Fishing ☐

_____
_____
_____

Foraging ☐

_____
_____
_____

Journey

Distance Covered

Trail Markers Used

Landmarks Sighted

Animal Prints

Map Sketch

Lat.   Long.

Party Member	Status	Injuries	Treatment

Date _____

Conditions

Weather

Terrain

Food Inventory

Rations ☐

_____
_____
_____
_____

Water ☐

Hunting ☐

_____
_____
_____

Fishing ☐

_____
_____
_____

Foraging ☐

_____
_____
_____

Journey

Distance Covered

Trail Markers Used

Landmarks Sighted

Animal Prints

Shelter

Shelter Constructed ☐

Type of Shelter

_____
_____
_____

Clothing/Coverings ☐
Waterproof ☐
Animal proof ☐
Sunproof ☐
Fire Started ☐

Map Sketch

Lat.   Long.

Party Member	Status	Injuries	Treatment

Date _____

Conditions

Weather

Terrain

Shelter

Shelter Constructed ☐

Type of Shelter

_____

_____

_____

Clothing/Coverings ☐

Waterproof ☐

Animal proof ☐

Sunproof ☐

Fire Started ☐

Food Inventory

Rations ☐

_____

_____

_____

_____

Water ☐

Hunting ☐

_____

_____

_____

Fishing ☐

_____

_____

_____

Foraging ☐

_____

_____

_____

Journey

Distance Covered

Trail Markers Used

Landmarks Sighted

Animal Prints

Map Sketch

Lat. _____ Long. _____

Party Member	Status	Injuries	Treatment

Date _____

Conditions

Weather

Terrain

Shelter

Shelter Constructed ☐

Type of Shelter

_____

_____

_____

Clothing/Coverings ☐
Waterproof ☐
Animal proof ☐
Sunproof ☐
Fire Started ☐

Food Inventory

Rations ☐

_____
_____
_____
_____

Water ☐
Hunting ☐

_____
_____
_____

Fishing ☐

_____
_____

Foraging ☐

_____
_____

Journey

Distance Covered

Trail Markers Used

Landmarks Sighted

Animal Prints

Map Sketch

Lat.   Long.

Party Member	Status	Injuries	Treatment

Date _____

Conditions

Weather

Terrain

Shelter

Shelter Constructed ☐

Type of Shelter

_____

_____

Clothing/Coverings ☐

Waterproof ☐

Animal proof ☐

Sunproof ☐

Fire Started ☐

Food Inventory

Rations ☐

_____
_____
_____
_____

Water ☐

Hunting ☐

_____
_____
_____

Fishing ☐

_____
_____

Foraging ☐

_____
_____

Journey

Distance Covered

Trail Markers Used

Landmarks Sighted

Animal Prints

Map Sketch

Lat.   Long.

Party Member	Status	Injuries	Treatment

Date _____

Conditions

Weather

Terrain

Shelter

Shelter Constructed ☐

Type of Shelter

_____

_____

Clothing/Coverings ☐

Waterproof ☐

Animal proof ☐

Sunproof ☐

Fire Started ☐

Food Inventory

Rations ☐

_____

_____

_____

_____

Water ☐

Hunting ☐

_____

_____

Fishing ☐

_____

_____

Foraging ☐

_____

_____

Journey

Distance Covered

Trail Markers Used

Landmarks Sighted

Animal Prints

Map Sketch

Lat.   Long.

Party Member	Status	Injuries	Treatment

Date _____

Conditions

Weather

Terrain

Shelter

Shelter Constructed ☐

Type of Shelter

_____

_____

_____

Clothing/Coverings ☐

Waterproof ☐

Animal proof ☐

Sunproof ☐

Fire Started ☐

Food Inventory

Rations ☐

_____

_____

_____

_____

Water ☐

Hunting ☐

_____

_____

_____

Fishing ☐

_____

_____

Foraging ☐

_____

_____

_____

Journey

Distance Covered

Trail Markers Used

Landmarks Sighted

Animal Prints

Map Sketch

Lat.   Long.

Party Member	Status	Injuries	Treatment

Date _____

Conditions

Weather

Terrain

Shelter

Shelter Constructed ☐

Type of Shelter

_____

_____

_____

Clothing/Coverings ☐

Waterproof ☐

Animal proof ☐

Sunproof ☐

Fire Started ☐

Food Inventory

Rations ☐

_____
_____
_____
_____
_____

Water ☐

Hunting ☐

_____
_____
_____

Fishing ☐

_____
_____
_____

Foraging ☐

_____
_____
_____

Journey

Distance Covered

Trail Markers Used

Landmarks Sighted

Animal Prints

Map Sketch

Lat.   Long.

Party Member	Status	Injuries	Treatment

Date _____

Conditions

Weather

Terrain

Shelter

Shelter Constructed ☐

Type of Shelter

_____

_____

_____

Clothing/Coverings ☐

Waterproof ☐

Animal proof ☐

Sunproof ☐

Fire Started ☐

Food Inventory

Rations ☐

_____

_____

_____

_____

Water ☐

Hunting ☐

_____

_____

Fishing ☐

_____

_____

_____

Foraging ☐

_____

_____

Journey

Distance Covered

Trail Markers Used

Landmarks Sighted

Animal Prints

Map Sketch

Lat. _____ Long. _____

Party Member	Status	Injuries	Treatment

Date _____

Conditions

Weather

Terrain

Shelter

Shelter Constructed ☐

Type of Shelter

_____

_____

_____

Clothing/Coverings ☐

Waterproof ☐

Animal proof ☐

Sunproof ☐

Fire Started ☐

Food Inventory

Rations ☐

_____
_____
_____
_____

Water ☐

Hunting ☐

_____
_____
_____

Fishing ☐

_____
_____
_____

Foraging ☐

_____
_____
_____

Journey

Distance Covered

Trail Markers Used

Landmarks Sighted

Animal Prints

Map Sketch

Lat. _____ Long. _____

Party Member	Status	Injuries	Treatment

Date _____

Conditions

Weather

Terrain

Shelter

Shelter Constructed ☐

Type of Shelter

_____

_____

_____

Clothing/Coverings ☐

Waterproof ☐

Animal proof ☐

Sunproof ☐

Fire Started ☐

Food Inventory

Rations ☐

_____

_____

_____

_____

Water ☐

Hunting ☐

_____

_____

Fishing ☐

_____

_____

Foraging ☐

_____

_____

Journey

Distance Covered

Trail Markers Used

Landmarks Sighted

Animal Prints

Map Sketch

Lat. ___   Long. ___

Party Member	Status	Injuries	Treatment

Date _____

Conditions

Weather

Terrain

Shelter

Shelter Constructed ☐

Type of Shelter

_____

_____

_____

Clothing/Coverings ☐

Waterproof ☐

Animal proof ☐

Sunproof ☐

Fire Started ☐

Food Inventory

Rations ☐

_____
_____
_____
_____

Water ☐

Hunting ☐

_____
_____
_____

Fishing ☐

_____
_____

Foraging ☐

_____
_____
_____

Journey

Distance Covered

Trail Markers Used

Landmarks Sighted

Animal Prints

Map Sketch

Lat.   Long.

Party Member	Status	Injuries	Treatment

Date _____

Conditions

Weather

Terrain

Food Inventory

Rations ☐

_____
_____
_____
_____

Water ☐

Hunting ☐

_____
_____
_____

Fishing ☐

_____
_____
_____

Foraging ☐

_____
_____
_____

Journey

Distance Covered

Trail Markers Used

Landmarks Sighted

Animal Prints

Shelter

Shelter Constructed ☐

Type of Shelter

_____
_____
_____

Clothing/Coverings ☐
Waterproof ☐
Animal proof ☐
Sunproof ☐
Fire Started ☐

Map Sketch

Lat.   Long.

Party Member	Status	Injuries	Treatment

Date _____

Conditions

Weather

Terrain

Shelter

Shelter Constructed ☐

Type of Shelter

_____

_____

_____

Clothing/Coverings ☐

Waterproof ☐

Animal proof ☐

Sunproof ☐

Fire Started ☐

Food Inventory

Rations ☐

_____
_____
_____
_____

Water ☐

Hunting ☐

_____
_____
_____

Fishing ☐

_____
_____
_____

Foraging ☐

_____
_____
_____

Journey

Distance Covered

Trail Markers Used

Landmarks Sighted

Animal Prints

Map Sketch

Lat. _____ Long. _____

Party Member	Status	Injuries	Treatment

Date _____

Conditions

Weather

Terrain

Shelter

Shelter Constructed ☐

Type of Shelter

_____

_____

_____

Clothing/Coverings ☐

Waterproof ☐

Animal proof ☐

Sunproof ☐

Fire Started ☐

Food Inventory

Rations ☐

_____

_____

_____

_____

Water ☐

Hunting ☐

_____

_____

_____

Fishing ☐

_____

_____

Foraging ☐

_____

_____

_____

Journey

Distance Covered

Trail Markers Used

Landmarks Sighted

Animal Prints

Map Sketch

Lat. _____ Long. _____

Party Member	Status	Injuries	Treatment

Date _____

Conditions

Weather

Terrain

Shelter

Shelter Constructed ☐

Type of Shelter

_____

_____

_____

Clothing/Coverings ☐

Waterproof ☐

Animal proof ☐

Sunproof ☐

Fire Started ☐

Food Inventory

Rations ☐

_____

_____

_____

_____

Water ☐

Hunting ☐

_____

_____

Fishing ☐

_____

_____

Foraging ☐

_____

_____

_____

Journey

Distance Covered

Trail Markers Used

Landmarks Sighted

Animal Prints

Map Sketch

Lat. _____ Long. _____

Party Member	Status	Injuries	Treatment

Date _____

Conditions

Weather

Terrain

Shelter

Shelter Constructed ☐

Type of Shelter

_____

_____

_____

Clothing/Coverings ☐

Waterproof ☐

Animal proof ☐

Sunproof ☐

Fire Started ☐

Food Inventory

Rations ☐

_____

_____

_____

_____

Water ☐

Hunting ☐

_____

_____

_____

Fishing ☐

_____

_____

Foraging ☐

_____

_____

Journey

Distance Covered

Trail Markers Used

Landmarks Sighted

Animal Prints

Map Sketch

Lat.   Long.

Party Member	Status	Injuries	Treatment

Date _____

Conditions

Weather

Terrain

Shelter

Shelter Constructed ☐

Type of Shelter

_____

_____

_____

Clothing/Coverings ☐

Waterproof ☐

Animal proof ☐

Sunproof ☐

Fire Started ☐

Food Inventory

Rations ☐

_____
_____
_____
_____

Water ☐

Hunting ☐

_____
_____
_____

Fishing ☐

_____
_____

Foraging ☐

_____
_____

Journey

Distance Covered

Trail Markers Used

Landmarks Sighted

Animal Prints

Map Sketch

Lat.   Long.

Party Member	Status	Injuries	Treatment

Date _____

Conditions

Weather

Terrain

Shelter

Shelter Constructed ☐

Type of Shelter

_____

_____

_____

Clothing/Coverings ☐

Waterproof ☐

Animal proof ☐

Sunproof ☐

Fire Started ☐

Food Inventory

Rations ☐

_____

_____

_____

_____

Water ☐

Hunting ☐

_____

_____

_____

Fishing ☐

_____

_____

_____

Foraging ☐

_____

_____

_____

Journey

Distance Covered

Trail Markers Used

Landmarks Sighted

Animal Prints

Map Sketch

Lat. _____ Long. _____

Party Member	Status	Injuries	Treatment

Date _____

Conditions

Weather

Terrain

Shelter

Shelter Constructed ☐

Type of Shelter

_____

_____

_____

Clothing/Coverings ☐

Waterproof ☐

Animal proof ☐

Sunproof ☐

Fire Started ☐

Food Inventory

Rations ☐

_____
_____
_____
_____
_____

Water ☐

Hunting ☐

_____
_____
_____

Fishing ☐

_____
_____
_____

Foraging ☐

_____
_____
_____

Journey

Distance Covered

Trail Markers Used

Landmarks Sighted

Animal Prints

Map Sketch

Lat.   Long.

Party Member	Status	Injuries	Treatment

Date _____

Conditions

Weather

Terrain

Shelter

Shelter Constructed ☐

Type of Shelter

_____

_____

_____

Clothing/Coverings ☐

Waterproof ☐

Animal proof ☐

Sunproof ☐

Fire Started ☐

Food Inventory

Rations ☐

_____

_____

_____

_____

Water ☐

Hunting ☐

_____

_____

_____

Fishing ☐

_____

_____

_____

_____

Foraging ☐

_____

_____

_____

Journey

Distance Covered

Trail Markers Used

Landmarks Sighted

Animal Prints

Map Sketch

Lat.   Long.

Party Member	Status	Injuries	Treatment

Date _____

Conditions

Weather

Terrain

Shelter

Shelter Constructed ☐

Type of Shelter

_____

_____

_____

Clothing/Coverings ☐

Waterproof ☐

Animal proof ☐

Sunproof ☐

Fire Started ☐

Food Inventory

Rations ☐

_____

_____

_____

_____

Water ☐

Hunting ☐

_____

_____

_____

Fishing ☐

_____

_____

_____

Foraging ☐

_____

_____

_____

Journey

Distance Covered

Trail Markers Used

Landmarks Sighted

Animal Prints

Map Sketch

Lat. _____ Long. _____

Party Member	Status	Injuries	Treatment

Date _____

Conditions

Weather

Terrain

Shelter

Shelter Constructed ☐

Type of Shelter

_____

_____

_____

Clothing/Coverings ☐

Waterproof ☐

Animal proof ☐

Sunproof ☐

Fire Started ☐

Food Inventory

Rations ☐

_____
_____
_____
_____

Water ☐

Hunting ☐

_____
_____
_____

Fishing ☐

_____
_____
_____

Foraging ☐

_____
_____
_____

Journey

Distance Covered

Trail Markers Used

Landmarks Sighted

Animal Prints

Map Sketch

Lat. Long.

Party Member	Status	Injuries	Treatment

Date _____

Conditions

Weather

Terrain

Shelter

Shelter Constructed ☐

Type of Shelter

_____

_____

_____

Clothing/Coverings ☐

Waterproof ☐

Animal proof ☐

Sunproof ☐

Fire Started ☐

Food Inventory

Rations ☐

_____
_____
_____
_____

Water ☐

Hunting ☐

_____
_____
_____

Fishing ☐

_____
_____
_____

Foraging ☐

_____
_____
_____

Journey

Distance Covered

Trail Markers Used

Landmarks Sighted

Animal Prints

Map Sketch

Lat. _____ Long. _____

Party Member	Status	Injuries	Treatment

Date _____

Conditions

Weather

Terrain

Shelter

Shelter Constructed ☐

Type of Shelter

_____

_____

Clothing/Coverings ☐

Waterproof ☐

Animal proof ☐

Sunproof ☐

Fire Started ☐

Food Inventory

Rations ☐

_____
_____
_____
_____

Water ☐

Hunting ☐

_____
_____
_____

Fishing ☐

_____
_____

Foraging ☐

_____
_____
_____

Map Sketch

Lat.   Long.

Journey

Distance Covered

Trail Markers Used

Landmarks Sighted

Animal Prints

Party Member	Status	Injuries	Treatment

Date _____

Conditions

Weather

Terrain

Shelter

Shelter Constructed ☐

Type of Shelter

_____
_____
_____

Clothing/Coverings ☐

Waterproof ☐

Animal proof ☐

Sunproof ☐

Fire Started ☐

Food Inventory

Rations ☐
_____
_____
_____
_____

Water ☐

Hunting ☐
_____
_____

Fishing ☐
_____
_____

Foraging ☐
_____
_____

Journey

Distance Covered

Trail Markers Used

Landmarks Sighted

Animal Prints

Map Sketch

Lat.   Long.

Party Member	Status	Injuries	Treatment

Date _____

Conditions

Weather

Terrain

Shelter

Shelter Constructed ☐

Type of Shelter

_____

_____

_____

Clothing/Coverings ☐

Waterproof ☐

Animal proof ☐

Sunproof ☐

Fire Started ☐

Food Inventory

Rations ☐

_____

_____

_____

_____

Water ☐

Hunting ☐

_____

_____

_____

Fishing ☐

_____

_____

Foraging ☐

_____

_____

Journey

Distance Covered

Trail Markers Used

Landmarks Sighted

Animal Prints

Map Sketch

Lat. _____ Long. _____

Party Member	Status	Injuries	Treatment

Date _____

Conditions

Weather

Terrain

Food Inventory

Rations ☐

_____

_____

_____

_____

Water ☐

Hunting ☐

_____

_____

_____

Fishing ☐

_____

_____

_____

Foraging ☐

_____

_____

_____

Journey

Distance Covered

Trail Markers Used

Landmarks Sighted

Animal Prints

Shelter

Shelter Constructed ☐

Type of Shelter

_____

_____

_____

Clothing/Coverings ☐

Waterproof ☐

Animal proof ☐

Sunproof ☐

Fire Started ☐

Map Sketch

Lat. _____ Long. _____

Party Member	Status	Injuries	Treatment

Date _____

Conditions

Weather

Terrain

Shelter

Shelter Constructed ☐

Type of Shelter

_____

_____

_____

Clothing/Coverings ☐

Waterproof ☐

Animal proof ☐

Sunproof ☐

Fire Started ☐

Food Inventory

Rations ☐

_____

_____

_____

_____

Water ☐

Hunting ☐

_____

_____

_____

Fishing ☐

_____

_____

Foraging ☐

_____

_____

_____

Journey

Distance Covered

Trail Markers Used

Landmarks Sighted

Animal Prints

Map Sketch

Lat. _____ Long. _____

Party Member	Status	Injuries	Treatment

Date _____

Conditions

Weather

Terrain

Shelter

Shelter Constructed ☐

Type of Shelter

_____

_____

_____

Clothing/Coverings ☐

Waterproof ☐

Animal proof ☐

Sunproof ☐

Fire Started ☐

Food Inventory

Rations ☐

_____
_____
_____
_____

Water ☐

Hunting ☐

_____
_____
_____

Fishing ☐

_____
_____
_____

Foraging ☐

_____
_____
_____

Journey

Distance Covered

Trail Markers Used

Landmarks Sighted

Animal Prints

Map Sketch

Lat.   Long.

Party Member	Status	Injuries	Treatment

Date _____

Conditions

Weather

Terrain

Shelter

Shelter Constructed ☐

Type of Shelter

_____

_____

_____

Clothing/Coverings ☐

Waterproof ☐

Animal proof ☐

Sunproof ☐

Fire Started ☐

Food Inventory

Rations ☐

_____
_____
_____
_____

Water ☐

Hunting ☐

_____
_____
_____

Fishing ☐

_____
_____
_____

Foraging ☐

_____
_____
_____

Journey

Distance Covered

Trail Markers Used

Landmarks Sighted

Animal Prints

Map Sketch

Lat.   Long.

Party Member	Status	Injuries	Treatment

Date _____

Conditions

Weather

Terrain

Shelter

Shelter Constructed ☐

Type of Shelter

_____

_____

_____

Clothing/Coverings ☐

Waterproof ☐

Animal proof ☐

Sunproof ☐

Fire Started ☐

Food Inventory

Rations ☐

_____
_____
_____
_____

Water ☐

Hunting ☐

_____
_____
_____

Fishing ☐

_____
_____
_____

Foraging ☐

_____
_____
_____

Journey

Distance Covered

Trail Markers Used

Landmarks Sighted

Animal Prints

Map Sketch

Lat.   Long.

Party Member	Status	Injuries	Treatment

Date _____

Conditions

Weather

Terrain

Shelter

Shelter Constructed ☐

Type of Shelter

_____

_____

_____

Clothing/Coverings ☐

Waterproof ☐

Animal proof ☐

Sunproof ☐

Fire Started ☐

Food Inventory

Rations ☐

_____

_____

_____

_____

Water ☐

Hunting ☐

_____

_____

_____

Fishing ☐

_____

_____

_____

Foraging ☐

_____

_____

_____

Journey

Distance Covered

Trail Markers Used

Landmarks Sighted

Animal Prints

Map Sketch

Lat. _____ Long. _____

Party Member	Status	Injuries	Treatment

Date _____

Conditions

Weather

Terrain

Shelter

Shelter Constructed ☐

Type of Shelter

_____

_____

_____

Clothing/Coverings ☐
Waterproof ☐
Animal proof ☐
Sunproof ☐
Fire Started ☐

Food Inventory

Rations ☐

_____
_____
_____
_____

Water ☐
Hunting ☐

_____
_____
_____

Fishing ☐

_____
_____
_____

Foraging ☐

_____
_____

Journey

Distance Covered

Trail Markers Used

Landmarks Sighted

Animal Prints

Map Sketch

Lat. _____ Long. _____

Party Member	Status	Injuries	Treatment

Date _____

Conditions

Weather

Terrain

Shelter

Shelter Constructed ☐

Type of Shelter

_____

_____

_____

Clothing/Coverings ☐

Waterproof ☐

Animal proof ☐

Sunproof ☐

Fire Started ☐

Food Inventory

Rations ☐

_____
_____
_____
_____

Water ☐

Hunting ☐

_____
_____
_____

Fishing ☐

_____
_____

Foraging ☐

_____
_____
_____

Journey

Distance Covered

Trail Markers Used

Landmarks Sighted

Animal Prints

Map Sketch

Lat. _____ Long. _____

Party Member	Status	Injuries	Treatment

Date _____

Conditions

Weather

Terrain

Shelter

Shelter Constructed ☐

Type of Shelter

_____

_____

Clothing/Coverings ☐

Waterproof ☐

Animal proof ☐

Sunproof ☐

Fire Started ☐

Food Inventory

Rations ☐

_____

_____

_____

_____

Water ☐

Hunting ☐

_____

_____

_____

Fishing ☐

_____

_____

_____

Foraging ☐

_____

_____

_____

Journey

Distance Covered

Trail Markers Used

Landmarks Sighted

Animal Prints

Map Sketch

Lat.   Long.

Party Member	Status	Injuries	Treatment

Date _____

Conditions

Weather

Terrain

Shelter

Shelter Constructed ☐

Type of Shelter

_____

_____

_____

Clothing/Coverings ☐

Waterproof ☐

Animal proof ☐

Sunproof ☐

Fire Started ☐

Food Inventory

Rations ☐

_____

_____

_____

_____

Water ☐

Hunting ☐

_____

_____

_____

Fishing ☐

_____

_____

_____

Foraging ☐

_____

_____

Journey

Distance Covered

Trail Markers Used

Landmarks Sighted

Animal Prints

Map Sketch

Lat. _____   Long. _____

Party Member	Status	Injuries	Treatment

Date _____

Conditions

Weather

Terrain

Shelter

Shelter Constructed ☐

Type of Shelter

_____

_____

Clothing/Coverings ☐

Waterproof ☐

Animal proof ☐

Sunproof ☐

Fire Started ☐

Map Sketch

Lat. _____ Long. _____

Food Inventory

Rations ☐

_____

_____

_____

_____

Water ☐

Hunting ☐

_____

_____

_____

Fishing ☐

_____

_____

_____

Foraging ☐

_____

_____

_____

Journey

Distance Covered

Trail Markers Used

Landmarks Sighted

Animal Prints

Party Member	Status	Injuries	Treatment

Date _____

Conditions

Weather

Terrain

Shelter

Shelter Constructed ☐

Type of Shelter

_____

_____

_____

Clothing/Coverings ☐

Waterproof ☐

Animal proof ☐

Sunproof ☐

Fire Started ☐

Food Inventory

Rations ☐

_____

_____

_____

_____

Water ☐

Hunting ☐

_____

_____

_____

Fishing ☐

_____

_____

Foraging ☐

_____

_____

_____

Journey

Distance Covered

Trail Markers Used

Landmarks Sighted

Animal Prints

Map Sketch

Lat. Long.

Party Member	Status	Injuries	Treatment

Date _____

Conditions

Weather

Terrain

Shelter

Shelter Constructed ☐

Type of Shelter

_____

_____

_____

Clothing/Coverings ☐

Waterproof ☐

Animal proof ☐

Sunproof ☐

Fire Started ☐

Food Inventory

Rations ☐

_____

_____

_____

_____

Water ☐

Hunting ☐

_____

_____

_____

Fishing ☐

_____

_____

_____

Foraging ☐

_____

_____

_____

Journey

Distance Covered

Trail Markers Used

Landmarks Sighted

Animal Prints

Map Sketch

Lat. _____ Long. _____

Party Member	Status	Injuries	Treatment

Date _____

Conditions

Weather

Terrain

Shelter

Shelter Constructed ☐

Type of Shelter

_____

_____

_____

Clothing/Coverings ☐

Waterproof ☐

Animal proof ☐

Sunproof ☐

Fire Started ☐

Food Inventory

Rations ☐

_____
_____
_____
_____

Water ☐

Hunting ☐

_____
_____
_____

Fishing ☐

_____
_____

Foraging ☐

_____
_____
_____

Journey

Distance Covered

Trail Markers Used

Landmarks Sighted

Animal Prints

Map Sketch

Lat. _____ Long. _____

Party Member	Status	Injuries	Treatment

Date _____

Conditions

Weather

Terrain

Shelter

Shelter Constructed ☐

Type of Shelter

_____

_____

_____

Clothing/Coverings ☐

Waterproof ☐

Animal proof ☐

Sunproof ☐

Fire Started ☐

Food Inventory

Rations ☐

_____

_____

_____

_____

Water ☐

Hunting ☐

_____

_____

Fishing ☐

_____

_____

Foraging ☐

_____

Journey

Distance Covered

Trail Markers Used

Landmarks Sighted

Animal Prints

Map Sketch

Lat. _____ Long. _____

Party Member	Status	Injuries	Treatment

Date _____

Conditions

Weather

Terrain

Shelter

Shelter Constructed ☐

Type of Shelter

_____

_____

_____

Clothing/Coverings ☐

Waterproof ☐

Animal proof ☐

Sunproof ☐

Fire Started ☐

Food Inventory

Rations ☐

_____

_____

_____

_____

Water ☐

Hunting ☐

_____

_____

_____

Fishing ☐

_____

_____

_____

Foraging ☐

_____

_____

_____

Journey

Distance Covered

Trail Markers Used

Landmarks Sighted

Animal Prints

Map Sketch

Lat. _____ Long. _____

Party Member	Status	Injuries	Treatment

Date _____

Conditions

Weather

Terrain

Shelter

Shelter Constructed ☐

Type of Shelter

_____

_____

_____

Clothing/Coverings ☐

Waterproof ☐

Animal proof ☐

Sunproof ☐

Fire Started ☐

Food Inventory

Rations ☐

_____
_____
_____
_____

Water ☐

Hunting ☐

_____
_____
_____

Fishing ☐

_____
_____
_____

Foraging ☐

_____
_____
_____

Journey

Distance Covered

Trail Markers Used

Landmarks Sighted

Animal Prints

Map Sketch

Lat. Long.

Party Member	Status	Injuries	Treatment

Date _____

Conditions

Weather

Terrain

Shelter

Shelter Constructed ☐

Type of Shelter

_____

_____

_____

Clothing/Coverings ☐

Waterproof ☐

Animal proof ☐

Sunproof ☐

Fire Started ☐

Food Inventory

Rations ☐

_____
_____
_____
_____

Water ☐

Hunting ☐

_____
_____
_____

Fishing ☐

_____
_____
_____

Foraging ☐

_____
_____
_____

Journey

Distance Covered

Trail Markers Used

Landmarks Sighted

Animal Prints

Map Sketch

Lat. _____ Long. _____

Party Member	Status	Injuries	Treatment

Date _____

Conditions

Weather

Terrain

Food Inventory

Rations ☐

_____
_____
_____
_____

Water ☐
Hunting ☐

_____
_____

Fishing ☐

_____
_____
_____

Foraging ☐

_____
_____

Journey

Distance Covered

Trail Markers Used

Landmarks Sighted

Animal Prints

Shelter

Shelter Constructed ☐

Type of Shelter

_____
_____
_____

Clothing/Coverings ☐
Waterproof ☐
Animal proof ☐
Sunproof ☐
Fire Started ☐

Map Sketch

Lat.   Long.

Party Member	Status	Injuries	Treatment

Date _____

Conditions

Weather

Terrain

Shelter

Shelter Constructed ☐

Type of Shelter

_____

_____

_____

Clothing/Coverings ☐

Waterproof ☐

Animal proof ☐

Sunproof ☐

Fire Started ☐

Food Inventory

Rations ☐

_____

_____

_____

_____

Water ☐

Hunting ☐

_____

_____

_____

Fishing ☐

_____

_____

_____

Foraging ☐

_____

_____

_____

Journey

Distance Covered

Trail Markers Used

Landmarks Sighted

Animal Prints

Map Sketch

Lat.   Long.

Party Member	Status	Injuries	Treatment

Date _____

Conditions

Weather

Terrain

Shelter

Shelter Constructed ☐

Type of Shelter

_____

_____

Clothing/Coverings ☐

Waterproof ☐

Animal proof ☐

Sunproof ☐

Fire Started ☐

Food Inventory

Rations ☐

_____

_____

_____

_____

Water ☐

Hunting ☐

_____

_____

_____

Fishing ☐

_____

_____

_____

Foraging ☐

_____

_____

_____

Journey

Distance Covered

Trail Markers Used

Landmarks Sighted

Animal Prints

Map Sketch

Lat.   Long.

Party Member	Status	Injuries	Treatment

Date _____

Conditions

Weather

Terrain

Shelter

Shelter Constructed ☐

Type of Shelter

_____

_____

_____

Clothing/Coverings ☐

Waterproof ☐

Animal proof ☐

Sunproof ☐

Fire Started ☐

Food Inventory

Rations ☐

_____
_____
_____
_____

Water ☐

Hunting ☐

_____
_____
_____

Fishing ☐

_____
_____
_____

Foraging ☐

_____
_____
_____

Journey

Distance Covered

Trail Markers Used

Landmarks Sighted

Animal Prints

Map Sketch

Lat. _____ Long. _____

Party Member	Status	Injuries	Treatment

Date _____

Conditions

Weather

Terrain

Shelter

Shelter Constructed ☐

Type of Shelter

_____

_____

_____

Clothing/Coverings ☐

Waterproof ☐

Animal proof ☐

Sunproof ☐

Fire Started ☐

Food Inventory

Rations ☐

_____

_____

_____

_____

Water ☐

Hunting ☐

_____

_____

_____

Fishing ☐

_____

_____

_____

Foraging ☐

_____

_____

Journey

Distance Covered

Trail Markers Used

Landmarks Sighted

Animal Prints

Map Sketch

Lat.   Long.

Party Member	Status	Injuries	Treatment

Date _____

Conditions

Weather

Terrain

Shelter

Shelter Constructed ☐

Type of Shelter

_____

_____

_____

Clothing/Coverings ☐

Waterproof ☐

Animal proof ☐

Sunproof ☐

Fire Started ☐

Food Inventory

Rations ☐

_____

_____

_____

_____

Water ☐

Hunting ☐

_____

_____

_____

Fishing ☐

_____

_____

Foraging ☐

_____

_____

_____

Journey

Distance Covered

Trail Markers Used

Landmarks Sighted

Animal Prints

Map Sketch

Lat.   Long.

Party Member	Status	Injuries	Treatment

Date _____

Conditions

Weather

Terrain

Shelter

Shelter Constructed ☐

Type of Shelter

_____

_____

_____

Clothing/Coverings ☐

Waterproof ☐

Animal proof ☐

Sunproof ☐

Fire Started ☐

Food Inventory

Rations ☐

_____
_____
_____
_____
_____

Water ☐

Hunting ☐

_____
_____
_____

Fishing ☐

_____
_____
_____

Foraging ☐

_____
_____
_____

Journey

Distance Covered

Trail Markers Used

Landmarks Sighted

Animal Prints

Map Sketch

Lat.   Long.

Party Member	Status	Injuries	Treatment

Date _____

Conditions

Weather

Terrain

Shelter

Shelter Constructed ☐

Type of Shelter

_____

_____

Clothing/Coverings ☐

Waterproof ☐

Animal proof ☐

Sunproof ☐

Fire Started ☐

Food Inventory

Rations ☐

_____
_____
_____
_____

Water ☐

Hunting ☐

_____
_____
_____

Fishing ☐

_____
_____
_____

Foraging ☐

_____
_____
_____

Journey

Distance Covered

Trail Markers Used

Landmarks Sighted

Animal Prints

Map Sketch

Lat.   Long.

Party Member	Status	Injuries	Treatment

Date _____

Conditions

Weather

Terrain

Shelter

Shelter Constructed ☐

Type of Shelter

_____

_____

_____

Clothing/Coverings ☐

Waterproof ☐

Animal proof ☐

Sunproof ☐

Fire Started ☐

Food Inventory

Rations ☐

_____

_____

_____

_____

Water ☐

Hunting ☐

_____

_____

_____

Fishing ☐

_____

_____

_____

Foraging ☐

_____

_____

_____

Journey

Distance Covered

Trail Markers Used

Landmarks Sighted

Animal Prints

Map Sketch

Lat. _____   Long. _____

Party Member	Status	Injuries	Treatment

Date _____

Conditions

Weather

Terrain

Shelter

Shelter Constructed ☐

Type of Shelter

_____

_____

_____

Clothing/Coverings ☐

Waterproof ☐

Animal proof ☐

Sunproof ☐

Fire Started ☐

Food Inventory

Rations ☐

_____

_____

_____

_____

Water ☐

Hunting ☐

_____

_____

_____

Fishing ☐

_____

_____

Foraging ☐

_____

_____

Journey

Distance Covered

Trail Markers Used

Landmarks Sighted

Animal Prints

Map Sketch

Lat.   Long.

Party Member	Status	Injuries	Treatment

Date _____

Conditions

Weather

Terrain

Shelter

Shelter Constructed ☐

Type of Shelter

_____

_____

_____

Clothing/Coverings ☐

Waterproof ☐

Animal proof ☐

Sunproof ☐

Fire Started ☐

Food Inventory

Rations ☐

_____

_____

_____

_____

Water ☐

Hunting ☐

_____

_____

_____

Fishing ☐

_____

_____

Foraging ☐

_____

_____

_____

Journey

Distance Covered

Trail Markers Used

Landmarks Sighted

Animal Prints

Map Sketch

Lat.   Long.

Party Member	Status	Injuries	Treatment

Date _____

Conditions

Weather

Terrain

Shelter

Shelter Constructed ☐

Type of Shelter

_____

_____

_____

Clothing/Coverings ☐

Waterproof ☐

Animal proof ☐

Sunproof ☐

Fire Started ☐

Food Inventory

Rations ☐

_____
_____
_____
_____

Water ☐

Hunting ☐

_____
_____
_____

Fishing ☐

_____
_____

Foraging ☐

_____
_____

Journey

Distance Covered

Trail Markers Used

Landmarks Sighted

Animal Prints

Map Sketch

Lat. _____ Long. _____

Party Member	Status	Injuries	Treatment

Date _____

Conditions

Weather

Terrain

Shelter

Shelter Constructed ☐

Type of Shelter

_____

_____

_____

Clothing/Coverings ☐

Waterproof ☐

Animal proof ☐

Sunproof ☐

Fire Started ☐

Food Inventory

Rations ☐

_____

_____

_____

_____

Water ☐

Hunting ☐

_____

_____

_____

Fishing ☐

_____

_____

_____

Foraging ☐

_____

_____

_____

Journey

Distance Covered

Trail Markers Used

Landmarks Sighted

Animal Prints

Map Sketch

Lat.   Long.

Party Member	Status	Injuries	Treatment

Date _____

Conditions

Weather

Terrain

Food Inventory

Rations ☐

_____
_____
_____
_____
_____

Water ☐

Hunting ☐

_____
_____
_____

Fishing ☐

_____
_____
_____

Foraging ☐

_____
_____
_____

Journey

Distance Covered

Trail Markers Used

Landmarks Sighted

Animal Prints

Shelter

Shelter Constructed ☐

Type of Shelter

_____
_____
_____

Clothing/Coverings ☐

Waterproof ☐

Animal proof ☐

Sunproof ☐

Fire Started ☐

Map Sketch

Lat. _____ Long. _____

Party Member	Status	Injuries	Treatment

Date _____

Conditions

Weather

Terrain

Shelter

Shelter Constructed ☐

Type of Shelter

_____

_____

_____

Clothing/Coverings ☐

Waterproof ☐

Animal proof ☐

Sunproof ☐

Fire Started ☐

Food Inventory

Rations ☐

_____
_____
_____
_____

Water ☐

Hunting ☐

_____
_____

Fishing ☐

_____
_____
_____

Foraging ☐

_____
_____

Journey

Distance Covered

Trail Markers Used

Landmarks Sighted

Animal Prints

Map Sketch

Lat.   Long.

Party Member	Status	Injuries	Treatment

Date _____

Conditions

Weather

Terrain

Shelter

Shelter Constructed ☐

Type of Shelter

_____

_____

_____

Clothing/Coverings ☐

Waterproof ☐

Animal proof ☐

Sunproof ☐

Fire Started ☐

Food Inventory

Rations ☐

_____
_____
_____
_____

Water ☐

Hunting ☐

_____
_____
_____

Fishing ☐

_____
_____
_____

Foraging ☐

_____
_____

Journey

Distance Covered

Trail Markers Used

Landmarks Sighted

Animal Prints

Map Sketch

Lat.   Long.

Party Member	Status	Injuries	Treatment

Date _____

Conditions

Weather

Terrain

Shelter

Shelter Constructed ☐

Type of Shelter

_____

_____

_____

Clothing/Coverings ☐

Waterproof ☐

Animal proof ☐

Sunproof ☐

Fire Started ☐

Food Inventory

Rations ☐

_____

_____

_____

_____

Water ☐

Hunting ☐

_____

_____

_____

Fishing ☐

_____

_____

Foraging ☐

_____

_____

_____

Journey

Distance Covered

Trail Markers Used

Landmarks Sighted

Animal Prints

Map Sketch

Lat.   Long.

Party Member	Status	Injuries	Treatment

Date _____

Conditions

Weather

Terrain

Shelter

Shelter Constructed ☐

Type of Shelter

_____

_____

_____

Clothing/Coverings ☐

Waterproof ☐

Animal proof ☐

Sunproof ☐

Fire Started ☐

Food Inventory

Rations ☐

_____
_____
_____
_____

Water ☐

Hunting ☐

_____
_____
_____

Fishing ☐

_____
_____

Foraging ☐

_____
_____
_____

Journey

Distance Covered

Trail Markers Used

Landmarks Sighted

Animal Prints

Map Sketch

Lat. _____ Long. _____

Party Member	Status	Injuries	Treatment

Date _____

Conditions

Weather

Terrain

Shelter

Shelter Constructed ☐

Type of Shelter

_____

_____

Clothing/Coverings ☐

Waterproof ☐

Animal proof ☐

Sunproof ☐

Fire Started ☐

Food Inventory

Rations ☐

_____

_____

_____

_____

Water ☐

Hunting ☐

_____

_____

Fishing ☐

_____

_____

Foraging ☐

_____

_____

Journey

Distance Covered

Trail Markers Used

Landmarks Sighted

Animal Prints

Map Sketch

Lat. _____   Long. _____

Party Member	Status	Injuries	Treatment

Date _____

Conditions

Weather

Terrain

Shelter

Shelter Constructed ☐

Type of Shelter

_____

_____

_____

Clothing/Coverings ☐

Waterproof ☐

Animal proof ☐

Sunproof ☐

Fire Started ☐

Food Inventory

Rations ☐

_____

_____

_____

_____

Water ☐

Hunting ☐

_____

_____

_____

Fishing ☐

_____

_____

_____

Foraging ☐

_____

_____

_____

Journey

Distance Covered

Trail Markers Used

Landmarks Sighted

Animal Prints

Map Sketch

Lat. _____ Long. _____

Party Member	Status	Injuries	Treatment

Date _____

Conditions

Weather

Terrain

Shelter

Shelter Constructed ☐

Type of Shelter

_____

_____

_____

Clothing/Coverings ☐

Waterproof ☐

Animal proof ☐

Sunproof ☐

Fire Started ☐

Food Inventory

Rations ☐

_____

_____

_____

_____

Water ☐

Hunting ☐

_____

_____

Fishing ☐

_____

_____

Foraging ☐

_____

_____

Journey

Distance Covered

Trail Markers Used

Landmarks Sighted

Animal Prints

Map Sketch

Lat. _____ Long. _____

Party Member	Status	Injuries	Treatment

Date _____

Conditions

Weather

Terrain

Shelter

Shelter Constructed ☐

Type of Shelter

_____

_____

_____

Clothing/Coverings ☐

Waterproof ☐

Animal proof ☐

Sunproof ☐

Fire Started ☐

Food Inventory

Rations ☐

_____

_____

_____

_____

Water ☐

Hunting ☐

_____

_____

_____

Fishing ☐

_____

_____

Foraging ☐

_____

_____

Journey

Distance Covered

Trail Markers Used

Landmarks Sighted

Animal Prints

Map Sketch

Lat.   Long.

Party Member	Status	Injuries	Treatment

Date _____

Conditions

Weather

Terrain

Shelter

Shelter Constructed ☐

Type of Shelter

_____

_____

_____

Clothing/Coverings ☐

Waterproof ☐

Animal proof ☐

Sunproof ☐

Fire Started ☐

Food Inventory

Rations ☐

_____

_____

_____

_____

Water ☐

Hunting ☐

_____

_____

_____

Fishing ☐

_____

_____

_____

Foraging ☐

_____

_____

_____

Journey

Distance Covered

Trail Markers Used

Landmarks Sighted

Animal Prints

Map Sketch

Lat.   Long.

Party Member	Status	Injuries	Treatment

Date _____

Conditions

Weather

Terrain

Shelter

Shelter Constructed ☐

Type of Shelter

_____

_____

_____

Clothing/Coverings ☐

Waterproof ☐

Animal proof ☐

Sunproof ☐

Fire Started ☐

Food Inventory

Rations ☐

_____
_____
_____
_____

Water ☐

Hunting ☐

_____
_____
_____

Fishing ☐

_____
_____

Foraging ☐

_____
_____

Journey

Distance Covered

Trail Markers Used

Landmarks Sighted

Animal Prints

Map Sketch

Lat. _____ Long. _____

Party Member	Status	Injuries	Treatment

Date _____

Conditions

Weather

Terrain

Shelter

Shelter Constructed ☐

Type of Shelter

_____

_____

_____

Clothing/Coverings ☐

Waterproof ☐

Animal proof ☐

Sunproof ☐

Fire Started ☐

Food Inventory

Rations ☐

_____

_____

_____

_____

Water ☐

Hunting ☐

_____

_____

_____

Fishing ☐

_____

_____

_____

Foraging ☐

_____

_____

_____

Journey

Distance Covered

Trail Markers Used

Landmarks Sighted

Animal Prints

Map Sketch

Lat. _____ Long. _____

Party Member	Status	Injuries	Treatment

Date _____

Conditions

Weather

Terrain

Food Inventory

Rations ☐

_____
_____
_____
_____

Water ☐

Hunting ☐

_____
_____
_____

Fishing ☐

_____
_____

Foraging ☐

_____
_____
_____

Journey

Distance Covered

Trail Markers Used

Landmarks Sighted

Animal Prints

Shelter

Shelter Constructed ☐

Type of Shelter

_____
_____
_____

Clothing/Coverings ☐

Waterproof ☐

Animal proof ☐

Sunproof ☐

Fire Started ☐

Map Sketch

Lat.   Long.

Party Member	Status	Injuries	Treatment

Date _____

Conditions

Weather

Terrain

Shelter

Shelter Constructed ☐

Type of Shelter

_____

_____

_____

Clothing/Coverings ☐

Waterproof ☐

Animal proof ☐

Sunproof ☐

Fire Started ☐

Food Inventory

Rations ☐

_____

_____

_____

_____

Water ☐

Hunting ☐

_____

_____

_____

Fishing ☐

_____

_____

_____

Foraging ☐

_____

_____

_____

Journey

Distance Covered

Trail Markers Used

Landmarks Sighted

Animal Prints

Map Sketch

Lat.   Long.

Party Member	Status	Injuries	Treatment

Date _____

Conditions

Weather

Terrain

Shelter

Shelter Constructed ☐

Type of Shelter

_____

_____

Clothing/Coverings ☐

Waterproof ☐

Animal proof ☐

Sunproof ☐

Fire Started ☐

Food Inventory

Rations ☐

_____

_____

_____

_____

Water ☐

Hunting ☐

_____

_____

_____

Fishing ☐

_____

_____

_____

Foraging ☐

_____

_____

_____

Journey

Distance Covered

Trail Markers Used

Landmarks Sighted

Animal Prints

Map Sketch

Lat.　　　Long.

Party Member	Status	Injuries	Treatment

Date _____

Conditions

Weather

Terrain

Shelter

Shelter Constructed ☐

Type of Shelter

_____

_____

_____

Clothing/Coverings ☐

Waterproof ☐

Animal proof ☐

Sunproof ☐

Fire Started ☐

Food Inventory

Rations ☐

_____

_____

_____

_____

Water ☐

Hunting ☐

_____

_____

_____

Fishing ☐

_____

_____

Foraging ☐

_____

_____

_____

Journey

Distance Covered

Trail Markers Used

Landmarks Sighted

Animal Prints

Map Sketch

Lat.   Long.

Party Member	Status	Injuries	Treatment

Date _____

Conditions

Weather

Terrain

Shelter

Shelter Constructed ☐

Type of Shelter

_____

_____

_____

Clothing/Coverings ☐

Waterproof ☐

Animal proof ☐

Sunproof ☐

Fire Started ☐

Food Inventory

Rations ☐

_____
_____
_____
_____

Water ☐

Hunting ☐

_____
_____
_____

Fishing ☐

_____
_____

Foraging ☐

_____
_____
_____

Journey

Distance Covered

Trail Markers Used

Landmarks Sighted

Animal Prints

Map Sketch

Lat.   Long.

Party Member	Status	Injuries	Treatment

Date _____

Conditions

Weather

Terrain

Shelter

Shelter Constructed ☐

Type of Shelter

_____

_____

Clothing/Coverings ☐

Waterproof ☐

Animal proof ☐

Sunproof ☐

Fire Started ☐

Food Inventory

Rations ☐

_____
_____
_____
_____

Water ☐

Hunting ☐

_____
_____
_____

Fishing ☐

_____
_____

Foraging ☐

_____
_____
_____

Map Sketch

Lat. _____ Long. _____

Journey

Distance Covered

Trail Markers Used

Landmarks Sighted

Animal Prints

Party Member	Status	Injuries	Treatment

Date _____

Conditions

Weather

Terrain

Food Inventory

Rations ☐

_____
_____
_____
_____

Water ☐
Hunting ☐

_____
_____

Fishing ☐

_____
_____

Foraging ☐

_____
_____

Journey

Distance Covered

Trail Markers Used

Landmarks Sighted

Animal Prints

Shelter

Shelter Constructed ☐

Type of Shelter

_____
_____

Clothing/Coverings ☐
Waterproof ☐
Animal proof ☐
Sunproof ☐
Fire Started ☐

Map Sketch

Lat. _____ Long. _____

Party Member	Status	Injuries	Treatment

Date _____

Conditions

Weather

Terrain

Shelter

Shelter Constructed ☐

Type of Shelter

_____

_____

_____

Clothing/Coverings ☐

Waterproof ☐

Animal proof ☐

Sunproof ☐

Fire Started ☐

Food Inventory

Rations ☐

_____

_____

_____

_____

Water ☐

Hunting ☐

_____

_____

_____

Fishing ☐

_____

_____

_____

Foraging ☐

_____

_____

Journey

Distance Covered

Trail Markers Used

Landmarks Sighted

Animal Prints

Map Sketch

Lat.   Long.

Party Member	Status	Injuries	Treatment

Date _____

Conditions

Weather

Terrain

Shelter

Shelter Constructed ☐

Type of Shelter

_____

_____

_____

Clothing/Coverings ☐

Waterproof ☐

Animal proof ☐

Sunproof ☐

Fire Started ☐

Food Inventory

Rations ☐

_____

_____

_____

_____

Water ☐

Hunting ☐

_____

_____

_____

Fishing ☐

_____

_____

Foraging ☐

_____

_____

_____

Journey

Distance Covered

Trail Markers Used

Landmarks Sighted

Animal Prints

Map Sketch

Lat. _____ Long. _____

Party Member	Status	Injuries	Treatment

Date _____

Conditions

Weather

Terrain

Shelter

Shelter Constructed ☐

Type of Shelter

_____

_____

_____

Clothing/Coverings ☐

Waterproof ☐

Animal proof ☐

Sunproof ☐

Fire Started ☐

Food Inventory

Rations ☐

_____

_____

_____

_____

Water ☐

Hunting ☐

_____

_____

_____

Fishing ☐

_____

_____

Foraging ☐

_____

_____

Journey

Distance Covered

Trail Markers Used

Landmarks Sighted

Animal Prints

Map Sketch

Lat.   Long.

Party Member	Status	Injuries	Treatment

Date _____

Conditions

Weather

Terrain

Shelter

Shelter Constructed ☐

Type of Shelter

_____

_____

_____

Clothing/Coverings ☐

Waterproof ☐

Animal proof ☐

Sunproof ☐

Fire Started ☐

Food Inventory

Rations ☐

_____

_____

_____

_____

Water ☐

Hunting ☐

_____

_____

_____

Fishing ☐

_____

_____

Foraging ☐

_____

_____

_____

Journey

Distance Covered

Trail Markers Used

Landmarks Sighted

Animal Prints

Map Sketch

Lat. _____ Long. _____

Party Member	Status	Injuries	Treatment

Date _____

Conditions

Weather

Terrain

Shelter

Shelter Constructed ☐

Type of Shelter

_____

_____

_____

Clothing/Coverings ☐

Waterproof ☐

Animal proof ☐

Sunproof ☐

Fire Started ☐

Food Inventory

Rations ☐

_____

_____

_____

_____

Water ☐

Hunting ☐

_____

_____

_____

Fishing ☐

_____

_____

_____

Foraging ☐

_____

_____

_____

Journey

Distance Covered

Trail Markers Used

Landmarks Sighted

Animal Prints

Map Sketch

Lat.   Long.

Party Member	Status	Injuries	Treatment

Date _____

Conditions

Weather

Terrain

Shelter

Shelter Constructed ☐

Type of Shelter

_____

_____

_____

Clothing/Coverings ☐

Waterproof ☐

Animal proof ☐

Sunproof ☐

Fire Started ☐

Food Inventory

Rations ☐

_____
_____
_____
_____

Water ☐

Hunting ☐

_____
_____
_____

Fishing ☐

_____
_____

Foraging ☐

_____
_____
_____

Map Sketch

Lat.   Long.

Journey

Distance Covered

Trail Markers Used

Landmarks Sighted

Animal Prints

Party Member	Status	Injuries	Treatment

Date _____

Conditions

Weather

Terrain

Shelter

Shelter Constructed ☐

Type of Shelter

_____

_____

Clothing/Coverings ☐

Waterproof ☐

Animal proof ☐

Sunproof ☐

Fire Started ☐

Food Inventory

Rations ☐

Water ☐

Hunting ☐

Fishing ☐

Foraging ☐

Journey

Distance Covered

Trail Markers Used

Landmarks Sighted

Animal Prints

Map Sketch

Lat.   Long.

Party Member	Status	Injuries	Treatment

Date _____

Conditions

Weather

Terrain

Shelter

Shelter Constructed ☐

Type of Shelter

_____

_____

_____

Clothing/Coverings ☐

Waterproof ☐

Animal proof ☐

Sunproof ☐

Fire Started ☐

Food Inventory

Rations ☐

_____
_____
_____
_____

Water ☐

Hunting ☐

_____
_____
_____

Fishing ☐

_____
_____
_____

Foraging ☐

_____
_____
_____

Journey

Distance Covered

Trail Markers Used

Landmarks Sighted

Animal Prints

Map Sketch

Lat. _____ Long. _____

Party Member	Status	Injuries	Treatment

Date _____

Conditions

Weather

Terrain

Shelter

Shelter Constructed ☐

Type of Shelter

_____

_____

_____

Clothing/Coverings ☐

Waterproof ☐

Animal proof ☐

Sunproof ☐

Fire Started ☐

Food Inventory

Rations ☐

_____
_____
_____
_____

Water ☐

Hunting ☐

_____
_____
_____

Fishing ☐

_____
_____
_____

Foraging ☐

_____
_____
_____

Journey

Distance Covered

Trail Markers Used

Landmarks Sighted

Animal Prints

Map Sketch

Lat. _____ Long. _____

Party Member	Status	Injuries	Treatment

Date _____

Conditions

Weather

Terrain

Shelter

Shelter Constructed ☐

Type of Shelter

_____

_____

_____

Clothing/Coverings ☐

Waterproof ☐

Animal proof ☐

Sunproof ☐

Fire Started ☐

Food Inventory

Rations ☐

_____
_____
_____
_____

Water ☐

Hunting ☐

_____
_____
_____

Fishing ☐

_____
_____

Foraging ☐

_____
_____
_____

Journey

Distance Covered

Trail Markers Used

Landmarks Sighted

Animal Prints

Map Sketch

Lat. _____ Long. _____

Party Member	Status	Injuries	Treatment

Date _____

Conditions

Weather

Terrain

Shelter

Shelter Constructed ☐

Type of Shelter

_____

_____

_____

Clothing/Coverings ☐

Waterproof ☐

Animal proof ☐

Sunproof ☐

Fire Started ☐

Food Inventory

Rations ☐

_____

_____

_____

_____

Water ☐

Hunting ☐

_____

_____

Fishing ☐

_____

_____

Foraging ☐

_____

_____

Journey

Distance Covered

Trail Markers Used

Landmarks Sighted

Animal Prints

Map Sketch

Lat. _____   Long. _____

Party Member	Status	Injuries	Treatment

Date _____

Conditions

Weather

Terrain

Shelter

Shelter Constructed ☐

Type of Shelter

_____

_____

_____

Clothing/Coverings ☐

Waterproof ☐

Animal proof ☐

Sunproof ☐

Fire Started ☐

Food Inventory

Rations ☐

_____

_____

_____

_____

Water ☐

Hunting ☐

_____

_____

_____

Fishing ☐

_____

_____

Foraging ☐

_____

_____

Journey

Distance Covered

Trail Markers Used

Landmarks Sighted

Animal Prints

Map Sketch

Lat. _____ Long. _____

Party Member	Status	Injuries	Treatment

Date _____

Conditions

Weather

Terrain

Shelter

Shelter Constructed ☐

Type of Shelter

_____

_____

_____

Clothing/Coverings ☐

Waterproof ☐

Animal proof ☐

Sunproof ☐

Fire Started ☐

Food Inventory

Rations ☐

_____
_____
_____
_____

Water ☐

Hunting ☐

_____
_____

Fishing ☐

_____
_____

Foraging ☐

_____
_____
_____

Journey

Distance Covered

Trail Markers Used

Landmarks Sighted

Animal Prints

Map Sketch

Lat.   Long.

Party Member	Status	Injuries	Treatment

Date _____

Conditions

Weather

Terrain

Shelter

Shelter Constructed ☐

Type of Shelter

_____

_____

_____

Clothing/Coverings ☐

Waterproof ☐

Animal proof ☐

Sunproof ☐

Fire Started ☐

Food Inventory

Rations ☐

_____

_____

_____

_____

Water ☐

Hunting ☐

_____

_____

_____

Fishing ☐

_____

_____

Foraging ☐

_____

_____

Journey

Distance Covered

Trail Markers Used

Landmarks Sighted

Animal Prints

Map Sketch

Lat.   Long.

Party Member	Status	Injuries	Treatment

Date _____

Conditions

Weather

Terrain

Shelter

Shelter Constructed ☐

Type of Shelter

_____

_____

_____

Clothing/Coverings ☐

Waterproof ☐

Animal proof ☐

Sunproof ☐

Fire Started ☐

Food Inventory

Rations ☐

_____
_____
_____
_____

Water ☐

Hunting ☐

_____
_____
_____

Fishing ☐

_____
_____
_____

Foraging ☐

_____
_____
_____

Journey

Distance Covered

Trail Markers Used

Landmarks Sighted

Animal Prints

Map Sketch

Lat.   Long.

Party Member	Status	Injuries	Treatment

Date _____

Conditions

Weather

Terrain

Shelter

Shelter Constructed ☐

Type of Shelter

_____

_____

_____

Clothing/Coverings ☐

Waterproof ☐

Animal proof ☐

Sunproof ☐

Fire Started ☐

Food Inventory

Rations ☐

_____

_____

_____

_____

Water ☐

Hunting ☐

_____

_____

_____

Fishing ☐

_____

_____

Foraging ☐

_____

_____

Journey

Distance Covered

Trail Markers Used

Landmarks Sighted

Animal Prints

Map Sketch

Lat. _____ Long. _____

Party Member	Status	Injuries	Treatment

Date _____

Conditions

Weather

Terrain

Shelter

Shelter Constructed ☐

Type of Shelter

_____

_____

_____

Clothing/Coverings ☐

Waterproof ☐

Animal proof ☐

Sunproof ☐

Fire Started ☐

Food Inventory

Rations ☐

_____
_____
_____
_____

Water ☐

Hunting ☐

_____
_____
_____

Fishing ☐

_____
_____
_____

Foraging ☐

_____
_____
_____

Journey

Distance Covered

Trail Markers Used

Landmarks Sighted

Animal Prints

Map Sketch

Lat.   Long.

Party Member	Status	Injuries	Treatment

Date _____

Conditions

Weather

Terrain

Shelter

Shelter Constructed ☐

Type of Shelter

_____

_____

Clothing/Coverings ☐

Waterproof ☐

Animal proof ☐

Sunproof ☐

Fire Started ☐

Food Inventory

Rations ☐

_____
_____
_____
_____

Water ☐

Hunting ☐

_____
_____

Fishing ☐

_____
_____

Foraging ☐

_____
_____

Journey

Distance Covered

Trail Markers Used

Landmarks Sighted

Animal Prints

Map Sketch

Lat.   Long.

Party Member	Status	Injuries	Treatment

Date _____

Conditions

Weather

Terrain

Shelter

Shelter Constructed ☐

Type of Shelter

_____

_____

_____

Clothing/Coverings ☐

Waterproof ☐

Animal proof ☐

Sunproof ☐

Fire Started ☐

Food Inventory

Rations ☐

_____
_____
_____
_____

Water ☐

Hunting ☐

_____
_____
_____

Fishing ☐

_____
_____

Foraging ☐

_____
_____

Journey

Distance Covered

Trail Markers Used

Landmarks Sighted

Animal Prints

Map Sketch

Lat.   Long.

Party Member	Status	Injuries	Treatment

Date _____

Conditions

Weather

Terrain

Shelter

Shelter Constructed ☐

Type of Shelter

_____

_____

Clothing/Coverings ☐
Waterproof ☐
Animal proof ☐
Sunproof ☐
Fire Started ☐

Food Inventory

Rations ☐

_____
_____
_____
_____

Water ☐
Hunting ☐

_____
_____
_____

Fishing ☐

_____
_____

Foraging ☐

_____
_____
_____

Journey

Distance Covered

Trail Markers Used

Landmarks Sighted

Animal Prints

Map Sketch

Lat.   Long.

Party Member	Status	Injuries	Treatment

Date _____

Conditions

Weather

Terrain

Shelter

Shelter Constructed ☐

Type of Shelter

_____

_____

_____

Clothing/Coverings ☐

Waterproof ☐

Animal proof ☐

Sunproof ☐

Fire Started ☐

Map Sketch

Lat.   Long.

Food Inventory

Rations ☐

_____

_____

_____

_____

Water ☐

Hunting ☐

_____

_____

_____

Fishing ☐

_____

_____

_____

Foraging ☐

_____

_____

Journey

Distance Covered

Trail Markers Used

Landmarks Sighted

Animal Prints

Party Member	Status	Injuries	Treatment

Date _____

Conditions

Weather

Terrain

Shelter

Shelter Constructed ☐

Type of Shelter

_____

_____

_____

Clothing/Coverings ☐

Waterproof ☐

Animal proof ☐

Sunproof ☐

Fire Started ☐

Food Inventory

Rations ☐

_____

_____

_____

_____

Water ☐

Hunting ☐

_____

_____

_____

Fishing ☐

_____

_____

Foraging ☐

_____

_____

Journey

Distance Covered

Trail Markers Used

Landmarks Sighted

Animal Prints

Map Sketch

Lat.   Long.

Party Member	Status	Injuries	Treatment

Date _____

Conditions

Weather

Terrain

Shelter

Shelter Constructed ☐

Type of Shelter

_____

_____

_____

Clothing/Coverings ☐

Waterproof ☐

Animal proof ☐

Sunproof ☐

Fire Started ☐

Food Inventory

Rations ☐

_____
_____
_____
_____

Water ☐

Hunting ☐

_____
_____
_____

Fishing ☐

_____
_____
_____

Foraging ☐

_____
_____
_____

Journey

Distance Covered

Trail Markers Used

Landmarks Sighted

Animal Prints

Map Sketch

Lat. _____   Long. _____

Party Member	Status	Injuries	Treatment

Date _____

Conditions

Weather

Terrain

Shelter

Shelter Constructed ☐

Type of Shelter

_____

_____

_____

Clothing/Coverings ☐

Waterproof ☐

Animal proof ☐

Sunproof ☐

Fire Started ☐

Food Inventory

Rations ☐

_____

_____

_____

_____

Water ☐

Hunting ☐

_____

_____

_____

Fishing ☐

_____

_____

_____

Foraging ☐

_____

_____

_____

Journey

Distance Covered

Trail Markers Used

Landmarks Sighted

Animal Prints

Map Sketch

Lat. _____ Long. _____

Party Member	Status	Injuries	Treatment

Date _____

Conditions

Weather

Terrain

Food Inventory

Rations ☐

_____
_____
_____
_____

Water ☐

Hunting ☐

_____
_____
_____

Fishing ☐

_____
_____

Foraging ☐

_____
_____
_____

Journey

Distance Covered

Trail Markers Used

Landmarks Sighted

Animal Prints

Shelter

Shelter Constructed ☐

Type of Shelter

_____
_____
_____

Clothing/Coverings ☐

Waterproof ☐

Animal proof ☐

Sunproof ☐

Fire Started ☐

Map Sketch

Lat.   Long.

Party Member	Status	Injuries	Treatment

Date _____

Conditions

Weather

Terrain

Shelter

Shelter Constructed ☐

Type of Shelter

_____

_____

Clothing/Coverings ☐

Waterproof ☐

Animal proof ☐

Sunproof ☐

Fire Started ☐

Food Inventory

Rations ☐

_____

_____

_____

_____

Water ☐

Hunting ☐

_____

_____

Fishing ☐

_____

_____

Foraging ☐

_____

_____

Journey

Distance Covered

Trail Markers Used

Landmarks Sighted

Animal Prints

Map Sketch

Lat. _____ Long. _____

Party Member	Status	Injuries	Treatment

www.ingramcontent.com/pod-product-compliance
Lightning Source LLC
Chambersburg PA
CBHW080559030426
42336CB00019B/3259